I Spy Nursery Rhymes

Written by Charlotte Raby
and Emily Guille-Marrett
Illustrated by Amanda Enright

Collins

2

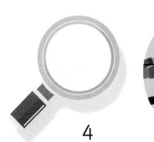

4

6

8

10

11

12

Can you say these nursery rhymes?

 Review: After reading

Read 1: Phonemic awareness

- Play 'find it!' by looking for the items in the small circles at the bottom of the pages, to build phonemic awareness. Choose an object or two per page and ask the children to find them in the illustration. Emphasise the initial sound of each word and then say the word. (e.g. *Can you find a shhh sheep?*)

- When they have found the object, ask the children to say the first sound of the word.

- Look together at pages 12 and 13. Can the children find all the places they have seen in the book? Can they remember what happened in each place? Look back in the book to check if necessary.

- Look at pages 14 and 15 together and ask the children to say the nursery rhymes. Draw attention to the rhyming sounds by emphasising the words that rhyme as you say them and point them out if the children are unsure.

Read 2: Vocabulary

- Encourage the children to hold the book and turn the pages.

- Spend time looking at the pictures and discussing them, drawing on any relevant experience or knowledge the children have. Encourage them to talk about what they can see in each picture, giving as much detail as they can. Expand the children's vocabulary by naming objects in the illustrations that they do not know.

- Sound-talk an object or two from the circles at the bottom of each page. (e.g. *Can you find the f-i-sh?*) Sound-talk but do not blend the word. When the children find the object, encourage them to blend the word.

Read 3: Comprehension

- Read the book again. Ask:
  - o Which one of the nursery rhymes do you like the most? Why?
  - o Can you think of another ending for that nursery rhyme?
- Enjoy singing nursery rhymes linked to the illustrations.